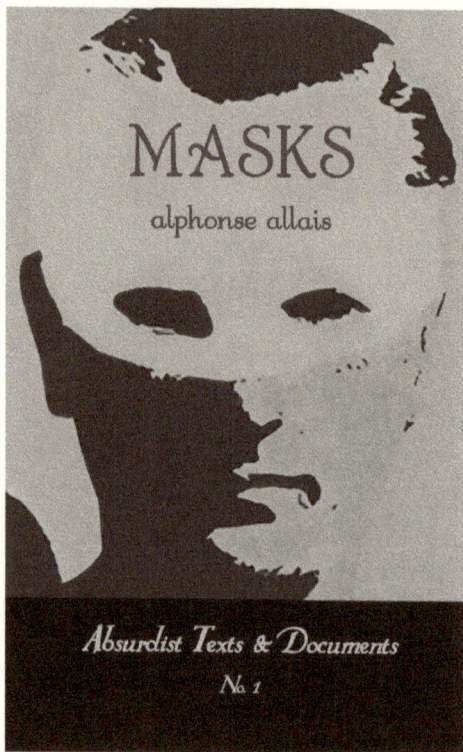

MASKS

alphonse allais

Absurdist Texts & Documents

№ 1

Alphonse Allais, *Masks*
The first Black Scat edition, published July 4, 2012.
[See page 13, item #1]

BLACK SCAT BOOKS:
BOOKS:
A BIBLIOGRAPHY
2012 · 2018

Compiled by Grace Murray

Journal of Experimental Fiction 79

JEF Books/Depth Charge Publishing
Aurora, Illinois

On the front cover: BSB clown logo designed by Norman Conquest, adapted from a 19th century French lantern catalog. Back cover: early poster advertising the Absurdist Texts & Documents series.

ISBN-13 978-1-884097-79-9
ISBN-10 1-884097-79-0
ISSN 1084-547X

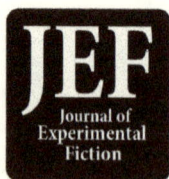

JEF
Journal of
Experimental
Fiction

JEF Books/Depth Charge Publishing
experimentalfiction.com
JEF Books are distributed to the trade by SPD: Small Press Distribution and to the academic journal market by EBSCO

The only concern of its kind in America

Contents

"Sublime Art & Literature" Marches On!

Black Scat Books was born on July, 4, 2012, in the San Francisco Bay Area. On that auspicious day, a limited edition chapbook came into the world: *Masks* by Alphonse Allais. This was publisher Norman Conquest's illustrated translation of the French humorist's pataphysical short story, "Un drame bien parisien." This booklet marked the inaugural volume in Black Scat's Absurdist Texts & Documents series, which set the tone for this unique, vibrant, and eccentric small press.

As of this writing, there are 34 titles in that series (plus 11 in its subset, Black Scat Classic Interim Editions), and all but three are out of print. These obscure volumes form the first two parts of this compilation. In all, I've referenced 113 titles—under several imprints—issued over the past six years. This includes novels, short fiction collections, poetry, works in translation, plays, humor, erotica, music, art, and anthologies—representing works by an international roster of artists and writers. It's a remarkable list for an indie press running on a shoestring budget. In fact, the publisher nearly ceased operation in 2016, but was saved by a successful fundraising campaign organized by author Carla M. Wilson.

This bibliography includes an addendum listing all 16 issues of the publisher's print journal, *Black Scat Review*. I've omitted 15 issues of the monthly digital magazine, *Le Scat Noir*, as well as over a dozen "Black Scat Broadsides"—a series of limited edition posters.

I wish to thank "président & fondateur" Norman Conquest for his invaluable help in annotating this list. I'm also extremely grateful to Eckhard Gerdes of JEF Books for making this bibliography available to collectors and fans.

Grace Murray
Amherst, Massachusetts
May, 2018

Abbreviations

AT&D = Absurdist Texts & Documents
BSB = Black Scat Books
c. = circa
comp. = compiled by
DOP = date of publication
DJ = dust jacket
ed. = edited by
Frontis = Frontispiece
Ltd Ed. = Limited Edition
n.d. = no date
NU = New Urge imprint
OP = out of print
pp. = pages
ppb =paperback
V. = Volume

Part I.

Absurdist Texts & Documents Series

1.
Alphonse Allais, *Masks*
Translated and designed by Norman Conquest
Fairfield, CA: Black Scat Books, July 4, 2012
Absurdist Texts & Documents No. 1
Limited to 50 copies; paper; illustrated; 26 pp.
[5¼ x 8¼ inches] OP

Revised & Expanded Edition: 2015
Introduction and notes on the text by Doug Skinner
50 pp. [5 x 8 inches] OP

Third Edition: 2018
[5 x 8 inches] OP

2.

Tom Whalen, *Doll with Chili Pepper*
Fairfield, CA: Black Scat Books, 2012
Absurdist Texts & Documents No. 2
Limited to 50 copies; paper; 30 pp.
[5¼ x 8¼ inches] OP

Note: cover photograph by Eleanor Bennett

3.

Derek Pell, *The Wonderful Wizard of Sade*
Fairfield, CA: Black Scat Books, 2012
Absurdist Texts & Documents No. 3
Limited to 50 copies; paper; illustrated; 30 pp.
[5¼ x 8¼ inches] OP

4.

Norman Conquest, ed., *Oulipo Pornobongo: Anthology of Erotic Wordplay*
Fairfield, CA: Black Scat Books, 2012
Absurdist Texts & Documents No. 4
Limited to 50 copies; paper; illustrated; 52 pp.
[5¼ x 8¼ inches] OP

Special Edition: 26 copies, lettered A-Z, with unique covers + signed/numbered fold-out erotic poster by artist Farewell Debut; plus Black Scat sticker. Shrink-wrapped.

5.

Ryan Forsythe, *If You Don't Read This the Terrorists Will Win*
Fairfield, CA: Black Scat Books, 2012
Absurdist Texts & Documents No. 5
Limited to 50 copies; paper; 30 pp.
[5¼ x 8¼ inches] OP

Note: Cropped photograph of Osama bin Laden appears on the front cover.

6.

Norman Conquest, *Snowdrop in Africa*
Fairfield, CA: Black Scat Books, 2012
Absurdist Texts & Documents No. 6
Limited to 50 copies; paper; illustrated; 30 pp.
[5¼ x 8¼ inches] OP

Note: First printing has three "clinamina" which were corrected in a second printing: caption beneath frontis illustration: "Chad" (Niger); page 8, last word "Chad" (Niger); page 23, 4th paragraph final word "ocean" (water). A *clinamen* in the Oulipian sense is a constraint which, in the author's words, "deviates from the norm in an arbitrary fashion so as not to be constrictive. Thus, the contstraint maintains its creative potential."

Special Edition: 6 signed copies with additional illustrations and blue front cover photograph of Bela Lugosi as wolf man in the film *Island of Lost Souls*; back cover: drawing of caped comic character in six sizes, plus the words "I" and "He" in large type. OP

7.

Samantha Memi, *Kate Moss & Other Heroines*
Fairfield, CA: Black Scat Books, 2012

Absurdist Texts & Documents No. 7
Limited to 50 copies; paper; 36 pp.
[5¼ x 8¼ inches] OP

Note: Statement on copyright page: "This edition marks the beginning of the second set of our AT&D series (six titles per set), and features a new colophon on the back cover to differentiate from #'s 1-6. Each title in the series is limited to 50 copies." However, later volumes in the series veered away from this classification of "sets," alternate colophons, and the 50 copy limit. For example, No. 30 was limited to 300 copies, while No. 33 featured the original colophon (paper dolls and scissors) on the back cover. The most recent release in the series, No. 34, has no edition limits.

8.

Isodore Isou, *Considerations on the Death and Burial of Tristan Tzara*
Translated from the French by Doug Skinner
Fairfield, CA: Black Scat Books, 2012
Absurdist Texts & Documents No. 8
Limited to 50 copies; paper; 28 pp.
[5¼ x 8¼ inches] OP

9.

Pierre Henri Cami, *A Cami Sampler*
Translated from the French by John Crombie
Illustrations by the author
Fairfield, CA: Black Scat Books, 2013
Absurdist Texts & Documents No. 9
Limited to 100 copies; paper; illustrated; 54 pp.
[5¼ x 8¼ inches] OP

10.
Pedro Carolino, *Cold in the Brain:
Poems by Pedro Carolino*
Annotated by Paul Forristal
Illustrated with 18th century woodcuts
Fairfield, CA: Black Scat Books, 2013
Absurdist Texts & Documents No. 10
Limited to 69 copies; paper; illustrated; 32 pp.
[5¼ x 8¼ inches] OP

11.
Alphonse Allais, *Captain Cap (V. I): Captain
Cap Before the Electorate*
Translated from the French by Doug Skinner
Illustrations by Doug Skinner
Fairfield, CA: Black Scat Books, 2013
Absurdist Texts & Documents No. 11
Limited to 125 copies; paper; illustrated; 60 pp.
[5¼ x 8¼ inches] OP

12.
Terry Southern, *Hot Heart of Boar & Other
Tastes*
Illustrations by Norman Conquest
Introduction by Nile Southern
Fairfield, CA: Black Scat Books, 2013
Absurdist Texts & Documents No. 12
Limited to 125 copies; paper; illustrated; 46 pp.
[5¼ x 8¼ inches] OP

Note: front cover has a photocopied image prepared by Terry Southern

13.

Anonymous, *Adventures in 'Pataphysics*
Fairfield, CA: Black Scat Books, 2012
Absurdist Texts & Documents No. 13
French text; edition limited to 60 copies; paper; illustrated, full color; 64 pp.
[5¼ x 8¼ inches] OP

———

Second Printing: 2015

Note: Front cover is identical to the first edition, but with a black bar at bottom, stating: "Second Printing"; also, preceding the word Pataphysics in the title is a single straight quote replacing an apostrophe on the original cover.

14.

Alphonse Allais, *Captain Cap (Vol. II): The Apparent Symbiosis Between the Boa and Giraffe*
Translated from the French by Doug Skinner
Illustrations by Doug Skinner
Fairfield, CA: Black Scat Books, 2013
Absurdist Texts & Documents No. 14

Limited to 125 copies; paper; illustrated; 104 pp.
[5¼ x 8¼ inches] OP

15.

Richard Kostelanetz, *The Works & Life of Kosty Richards: An American Career*
Fairfield, CA: Black Scat Books, 2013
Absurdist Texts & Documents No. 15
Limited to 125 copies; paper; 74 pp.
[5¼ x 8¼ inches] OP

16.
G. Mackenzie Bacon, M.D. *Wasted Energies,
Baffled Thoughts: On the Writing of the Insane*
Fairfield, CA: Black Scat Books, 2013
Absurdist Texts & Documents No. 16
Limited to 60 copies; paper; illustrated, color; 28 pp.
[5¼ x 8¼ inches]   OP

17.
Alphonse Allais, *Captain Cap (Vol. III). The
Antifilter & Other Inventions*
Translated from the French by Doug Skinner
With illustrations by Doug Skinner
Fairfield, CA: Black Scat Books, 2013
Absurdist Texts & Documents No. 17
Limited to 125 copies; paper; illustrated; 110 pp.
[5¼ x 8¼ inches]   OP

18.
Farewell Debut, *Blink: Visual Antiphonies*
Fairfield, CA: Black Scat Books, 2013
Absurdist Texts & Documents No. 18
Limited to 100 copies, paper; full color; 106 pp.
[5¼ x 8¼ inches]   OP

19.
Tom Whalen, *Hotel Ortolan*
Photographs by Michel Varisco
Fairfield, CA: Black Scat Books, 2013
Absurdist Texts & Documents No. 19

Limited to 125 copies; paper; b/w; 44 pp.
[5¼ x 8¼ inches]   OP

20.
Alphonse Allais, *Captain Cap (Vol. IV): The Sanatorium of the Future*
Translated from the French by Doug Skinner
With Illustrations by Doug Skinner
Fairfield, CA: Black Scat Book, 2013
Absurdist Texts & Documents No. 20
Limited to 125 copies; paper; illustrated; 84 pp.
[5¼ x 8¼] OP

21.
Peppo Bianchessi, *Contemporary Art for Rich Kids*
Illustrated by Peppo Bianchessi
Fairfield, CA: Black Scat Books, 2013
Absurdist Texts & Documents No. 21
Limited to 125 copies; paper; color; 64 pp.
[5¼ x 8¼] OP

22.
Honoré de Balzac, *Waiting for Godeau*
Translated from the French by Mark Axelrod
Fairfield, CA: Black Scat Books, 2013
Absurdist Texts & Documents No. 22
Limited to 250 copies; paper; 138 pp.
[5¼ x 8¼] OP

Note: Includes a previously unpublished letter by Samuel Beckett to the translator.

23.

Gisèle Prassinos, *Surrealist Texts*
Translated from the French by Ellen Nations
Illustrations by Bruce Hutchinson
Fairfield, CA: Black Scat Books, 2014
Absurdist Texts & Documents No. 23
Limited to 85 copies; paper; illustrated; 56 pp.
[5¼ x 8¼ inches]   OP

Excerpt from an extensive review by Lucina Schell in *Reading in Translation*: "Nations's translations admirably resist the urge to clarify or normalize Prassinos's surrealist prose. Complemented by Bruce Hutchinson's beautiful watercolors in a limited edition of only 85 copies, *Surrealist Texts* makes a lovely gift for connoisseurs of surrealism."

24.

Doug Skinner, comp., *Merde à La Belle Époque: Scatological Texts*
Translated from the French by Doug Skinner
Fairfield, CA: Black Scat Books, 2014
Absurdist Texts & Documents No. 24
Limited to 310 copies + 10 copies, signed & numbered, with a drawing by Doug Skinner; paper; 48 pp.
[5¼ x 8¼ inches]   OP

Contributors: Alphonse Allais, George Auriol, Georges Courteline, Edmond Haraucourt, Vincent Hyspa, Maurice Mac-Nab, and Erik Satie.

25.

Judson Hamilton, *The Sugar Numbers*
Fairfield, CA: Black Scat Books, 2014
Absurdist Texts & Documents No. 25
Limited to 150 copies; paper; 60 pp.
[5¼ x 8¼] OP

Note: cover art by Ievgen Kharuk

26.
Edward D. Wood, *Selected Poems of Edward D. Wood, Jr.*
Fairfield, CA: Black Scat Books, 2014
Absurdist Texts & Documents No. 26
Limited to 99 copies; paper; 28 pp.
[5¼ x 8¼ inches]   OP

27.
Norman Conquest, *Rear Windows: An Inside Look at Fifty Film Noir Classics*
Introduction by Robert Wexelblatt
Fairfield, CA: Black Scat Books, 2014
Absurdist Texts & Documents No. 27
Paper; illustrated; 70 pp.
[5¼ x 8¼ inches] OP

———
Second Edition: 2018
[5 x 8 inches]

Note: The front cover is unique and features a still photograph from the Hitchcock film *Rear Window* and states "Second Edition" at bottom.

28.
David R. Slavit, *Walloomsac: A Week on the River*
Fairfield, CA: Black Scat Books, 2014
Absurdist Texts & Documents No. 28
Paper; 88 pp.
[5¼ x 8¼ inches]   OP

29.
Norman Conquest, ed., *Oulipo Pornobongo 3:
Anthology of Erotic Wordplay*
Fairfield, CA: Black Scat Books, 2014
Absurdist Texts & Documents No. 29
Limited to 300 copies; Illustrated; paper; 58 pp.
[5¼ x 8¼ inches]   OP

30.
Jason E. Rolfe, *An Inconvenient Corpse*
Fairfield, CA: Black Scat Books, 2014
Absurdist Texts & Documents No. 30
Limited to 300 copies; paper, 66 pp.
[5¼ x 8¼ inches]   OP

31.
Doug Skinner, *Horoscrapes*
Fairfield, CA: Black Scat Books, 2014
Absurdist Texts & Documents No. 31
Paper; 66 pp.
[5¼ x 8¼ inches]   OP

Note: copyright page states "First Printing." Number of copies unknown.

32.
Karl Waldmann, comp., *True Crime:
The People vs. Rrose Sélavy*
Guerneville, CA: Black Scat Books, 2016
Absurdist Texts & Documents No. 32
Illustrated; paper; 38 pp.
[5¼ x 8¼ inches]   OP

33.
Paulo Brito, *Sons of Man*
Preface by Mercie Pedro e Silva
Guerneville, CA: Black Scat Books, 2017
Absurdist Texts & Documents No. 33
Illustrated, color collages; paper; 54 pp.
[5¼ x 8¼ inches] OP

34.
E. V. Lucas & George Morrow, *What a Life!*
Guerneville, CA: Black Scat Books, 2018
Absurdist Texts & Documents No. 34
Trade ppb; illustrated; 134 pp.
[5 x 8 inches]

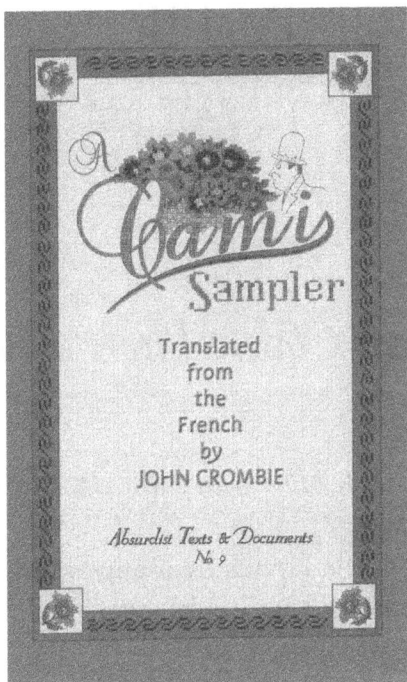

Pierre Henri Cami, *A Cami Sampler* (2013)
[See page 16, item #9]

Part II.

Black Scat Classic Interim Editions

35.
Alphonse Allais, *How I Became an Idiot by Francisque Sarcey*
Translated from the French by Doug Skinner
Fairfield, CA: Black Scat Books, 2013
Black Scat Classic Interim Edition No. 00
Limited to 60 copies; paper; 38 pp.
[5¼ x 8¼ inches] OP

Note: Title page features Sarcey's name crossed out, with Allais's name hand-written in.

36.
Poggio Bracciolini, *The Facetiae Erotica of Poggio*
Cover art and design by Jana Vukovic
Fairfield, CA: Black Scat Books, 2013
Black Scat Classic Interim Edition No. 01
Limited to 69 copies; paper; 114 pp.,
[5¼ x 8¼ inches] OP

37.
Derek Pell, *Doctor Bey's Suicide Guidebook*
Fairfield, CA: Black Scat Books, 2013
Black Scat Classic Interim Edition No. 02
Reprint; illustrated; limited to 85 copies; paper; 114 pp.
[5¼ x 8¼ inches] OP

Note: While I was in high school, I discovered a copy of the original edition
(Dodd, Mead & Co.: 1977)—loved it and eventually found Black Scat.

38.
Norman Conquest, ed., *Oulipo Pornobongo 2*
Fairfield, CA: Black Scat Books, 2013
Black Scat Classic Interim Edition No. 03
Paper; illustrated, color; saddle-stitched, 48 pp.
[5¼ x 8¼ inches] OP

39.
Monika Mori, *Moo Nudes*
Paintings by Monika Mori
Fairfield, CA: Black Scat Books, 2013
Black Scat Classic Interim Edition No. 04
Limited to 125 copies; paper; illustrated; 64 pp.,
[5¼ x 8¼ inches] OP

40.
Opal Louis Nations, *Embryo World & Others
Stripped Bare*
Fairfield, CA: Black Scat Books, 2013
Black Scat Classic Interim Edition No. 05
Limited to 125 copies; paper; illustrated, full color

collages; 52 pp.

[5¼ x 8¼ inches] OP

——

Second Printing: 2015
Limited to 100 copies; OP

Note: Brown bar at bottom of front cover states "Second Printing."

41.
Eckhard Gerdes, *'S A Bird*
Fairfield, CA: Black Scat Books, 2013
Black Scat Classic Interim Edition No. 06
Limited to 100 copies; paper; illustrated; 68 pp.
[5¼ x 8¼ inches] OP

42.
Robert Wexelblatt, *The Derangement of Jules Torquemal*
Fairfield, CA: Black Scat Books, 2014
Black Scat Classic Interim Edition No. 07
Limited to 100 copies; paper; 44 pp.
[5¼ x 8¼ inches] OP

43.
Allan Bealy, *Mud Bath*
Fairfield, CA: Black Scat Books, 2014
Black Scat Classic Interim Edition No. 08
Limited to 100 copies; paper; illustrated; color, collages; 68 pp.
[5¼ x 8¼ inches] OP

44.
Frank Pulaski, *Women That Don't Exist*
Fairfield, CA: Black Scat Books, 2014
Black Scat Classic Interim Edition No. 09
Limited to 100 copies; paper; illustrated; 63 pp.
[5¼ x 8¼ inches] OP

45.
Paul Rosheim, *Fishslices*
Fairfield, CA: Black Scat Books, 2014
Black Scat Classic Interim Edition No. 10
Limited to 125 copies; paper; illustrated; 36 pp.
[5¼ x 8¼ inches] OP

Note: This is a reprint of the revised and expanded edition published by
Obscure Publications in 2003.

Part III.

Black Scat Books

46.
Norman Conquest, *A Beginner's Guide to Art Deconstruction*
Introduction by Edward H. Hoage
Fairfield, CA: Black Scat Books, 2012
Paper; 26 pp.
[5¼ x 8¼ inches] OP

Note: No edition limit stated, but only 50 copies were printed. Plain, glossy red covers with text: "REVISED AND EXPANDED EDITION." This expanded version includes a part 5: "Weapons of Mass Deconstruction (WMDs)." Copyright page has DOP: "August, 2012." The original edition was published by Permeable Press (San Francisco: 1995) It was reprinted under the title *A Beginner's Guide to Art Deconstruction & Other Works* (Obscure Publications: 2007)

47.
Farewell Debut, *The Two Loves of Nunny*
Fairfield, CA: Black Scat Books, 2012
DOP: August 11, 2012
Full color; hardcover with DJ; 32 pp.
[7 x 7 inches] OP

Note: This is the sole hardcover edition issued by the publisher.

48.
Michael Leigh, *The Best of Christmas Catalogues*
Fairfield, CA: Black Scat Books, 2012
DOP: September 22, 2012
Trade ppb; 124 pp.
[6 x 0.3 x 9] OP

49.
Norman Conquest and Michael Leigh, *It's Fun to Be Rich in America*
Fairfield, CA: Beuyscout Editions /Black Scat, 2012
Paper; illustrated, collages; saddle-stitched 40 pp.
[5¼ x 8¼ inches] OP

———

Second Printing: 2012
OP

Note: The second printing has a unique cover with red and black design resembling a vampire. Includes a blurb on front by Tom Whalen: *"...a great goddamn, brilliant, sorrowful book."*

50.
Norman Conquest, *The Neglected Works of Norman Conquest*
Fairfield, CA: Black Scat Books, 2012
DOP: September 26, 2012
Paper; 68 pp.
[6 x 0.2 x 9 inches] OP

51.

Monika Mori, *Shattered Rainbow*
Fairfield, CA: Black Scat Books, 2012
DOP: November 29, 2012
Full color; paper; 32 pp.
[8.5 x 0.1 x 8.5 inches] OP

52.

Norman Conquest, *Don't worry, it's not about hats*
Fairfield, CA: Black Scat Books, 2012
Paper; color illustrations; 28 pp.
Limited to 50 copies
[5¼ x 8¼ inches] OP

Note: Copyright page states "FIRST EDITION." Mustard-colored glossy
covers. A second printing was issued (n.d.) with white covers

53.

Opal Louis Nations, *The Complete Unabridged Lexicon*
Fairfield, CA: Black Scat Books, 2012
DOP: December 30, 2012
Trade ppb; 128 pp.
[6 x 0.3 x 9 inches]

54.

Alain Arias-Mission, *The Man Who Walked On Air & Other Tales of Innocence*
Fairfield, CA: Black Scat Books, 2013
DOP: January 16, 2013

Trade ppb; 194 pp.
[6 x 0.5 x 9 inches]

55.
M. Kasper, *Kirghiz Steppes: Accumulated Verbo-visuals*
Fairfield, CA: Black Scat Books, 2013
DOP: March 5, 2013
Paper; illustrated; 82 pp.
Limited to 150 copies
[6 x 0.2 x 9 inches] OP

56.
C. S. Hibbard, *The Other Side: The Shocking Truth Behind 100 Classic Paintings*
Foreword by Paul Forristal
Fairfield, CA: Black Scat Books, 2013
DOP: April 16, 2013
Trade ppb; illus. w/ color photographs, 110 pp.
[6 x 0.3 x 9 inches] OP

57.
John Nickle, *Nickle Noir: The Art of John Nickle*
With an introduction by the artist
Fairfield, CA: Black Scat Books, 2013
DOP: May 17, 2013
Trade ppb; full color reproductions, 144 pp.
Limited to 150 copies
[6 x 0.3 x 9 inches] OP

58.

Alain Arias-Mission, *Tintin Meets the Dragon Queen in The Return of the Maya to Manhattan*
Fairfield, CA: Black Scat Books, 2013
DOP: September 15, 2013
Trade ppb; 260 pp.
[6 x 0.6 x 9 inches]

59.

Alphonse Allais, *Captain Cap: His Adventures, His Ideas, His Drinks*
Translated by Doug Skinner
With illustrations and notes by Doug Skinner
Fairfield, CA: Black Scat Books, 2013
DOP: October 8, 2013
Trade ppb; illustrated; 370 pp.
[6 x 0.9 x 9 inches]

Note: Portions of this translation first appeared in four volumes of the Absurdist Texts & Documents Series, Chapter XXII appeared in *Black Scat Review #5*, This trade edition includes eight uncollected stories and an appendix of rare historical pictures.

60.

Yuriy Tarnawsky, *Crocodile Smiles: Short Shrift Fictions*
Fairfield, CA: Black Scat Books, 2014
DOP: June 2, 2014
Trade ppb; 118 pp.
[6 x 0.3 x 9 inches]
Note: "The Haircut" first appeared in slightly different form in *Black Scat*

Review #4 "Dead Darling" first appeared in slightly different form in *Black Scat Review #1* and was reprinted with minor changes in *Best European Fiction 2014*, Dalkey Archive Press.

61.
Doug Skinner, *The Unknown Adjective & Other Stories*
Fairfield, CA: Black Scat Books, 2014
DOP: June 28, 2014
Trade ppb; illustrated; 112 pp.
[8 x 0.3 x 10 inches]

62.
Tom Whalen, *The Straw That Broke*
Fairfield, CA: Black Scat Books, 2014
DOP: July 30, 2014
Trade ppb; 172 pp.
[6 x 0.4 x 9 inches]

63.
Terri Lloyd and Norman Conquest, *The Little Red Book of Commie Porn*
Fairfield, CA: Black Scat Books, 2014
DOP: August 3, 2014
Limited to 100 copies; paper; illustrated, color; 50 pp.
[5¼ x 8¼ inches] OP

64.
Alphonse Allais, *Selected Plays of Alphonse Allais*
Translated and compiled by Doug Skinner
Fairfield, CA: Black Scat Books, 2014
DOP: September 8, 2014

"First Publication in English"
Trade pbk; illustrations; 124 pp.
[6 x 0.3 x 9 inches]

Note: Includes appendix of scarce photographs from the Paris production of *Le Pauvre Bougre et Le Bon Génie.* Copyright page states: "First Edition."

65.
Norman Conquest, *Fervent SFdical: Selected Capchas*
Fairfield, CA: Black Scat Books, 2014
26 copies printed; paper; 68 pp.
[5¼ x 8¼ inches] OP

66.
Suzanne Burns, *Sweet and Vicious*
Fairfield, CA: Black Scat Books, 2014
DOP: October 13, 2014
Trade ppb; 166 pp.
[6 x 0.4 x 9 inches]

Note: An excerpt from the novel originally appeared in *Black Scat Review* #8.

67.
Opal Louis Nations, *Sensational Nightingales: The Story of Joseph "Jo Jo" Wallace & the Early Days of the Sensational Nightingales*
Fairfield, CA: Black Scat Books, 2014
DOP: November 7, 2014
Trade ppb; illustrated; 146 pp.
[6 x 0.3 x 9 inches]
Note: Published as a "Scat Trax" edition, an imprint of Black Scat Books

Includes 40 pages of rare b/w photographs.

68.

Opal Louis Nations, *Brushes with Music: with Strokes in 1960s British Rock*
Fairfield, CA: Black Scat Books, 2014
DOP: December 3, 2014
Paper; 64 pp.
[6 x 0.2 x 9 inches]

Note: Published under the Scat Trax imprint.

69.

Norman Conquest, *Burn This Book!: Matchbook Art*
Fairfield, CA: Black Scat Books, 2015
Pamphlet; illustrated in full color; 28 pp.
[5¼ x 8¼] OP

Note: # of copies unknown. A digital edition (2014) can be viewed online at Issuu: https://issuu.com/normanconquest/docs/burn_this_book

70.

Richard Kostelanetz, *Gustave's Pocket Dictionary*
Bilingual edition
Guerneville, CA: Black Scat Books, 2015
DOP: November 4, 2015
Trade ppb; 190 pp.
[5.1 x 0.5 x 7.8 inches]

Note: An excerpt from this work originally appeared in *Black Scat Review* #11.

71.
Edith Doove, *Mince* (poems)
Guerneville, CA: Black Scat Books, 2015
DOP: January 31, 2015
Limited to 300 copies; paper; 28 pp.
OP

Note: Cover photograph by the author.

72.
Alphonse Allais, *The Squadron's Umbrella*
Translated from the French by Doug Skinner
With illustrations, notes, and an introduction by
Doug Skinner
Guerneville, CA: Black Scat Books, 2015
DOP: March 4, 2015
Trade ppb; illustrated, 160 pp.
[6 x 0.4 x 9 inches]

Note: The collection was originally published in France in 1893 under the
title *Le parapluie de l'escouade*. First publication in English.

73.
Doug Rice, *An Erotics of Seeing*
Guerneville, CA: Black Scat Books, 2015
DOP: March 9, 2015
Limited to 300 copies; Paper; illustrated with b/w
photographs; 64 pp.
[5¼ x 8¼ inches] OP

74.
Pierre-Corneille de Blessebois, *The Zombie of Great Peru or The Countess of Cocagne*
With a preface by Guillaume Apollinaire
Translated from the French by Doug Skinner
Guerneville, CA: Black Scat Books, 2015
DOP: April 2, 2015
Trade ppb; 146 pp.
[5.1 x 0.4 x 7.8 inches]

75.
Mark Axelrod, *Dante's Foil & Other Sporting Tales*
Guerneville, CA: Black Scat Books, 2015
DOP: April 29, 2015
Trade ppb; 150 pp.
[6 x 0.4 x 9 inches]

76.
Alain Arias-Mission, *Comic Book*
Guerneville, CA: Black Scat Books, 2015
DOP: June 9, 2015
Trade ppb; 170 pp.
[5.1 x 0.4 x 7.8 inches]

77.
Doug Skinner, *The Doug Skinner Dossier*
Guerneville, CA: Black Scat Books, 2015
DOP: July 5, 2015
Trade ppb; 248 pp.
[5.1 x 0.6 x 7.8 inches]

78.

Carla M. Wilson, *Impossible Conversations*
Guerneville, CA: Black Scat Books, 2015
DOP: August 2, 2015
Trade ppb; 220 pp.
[6 x 0.6 x 9 inches]

79.

Alphonse Allais, *The Blaireau Affair*
Translated by Doug Skinner
With an introduction by Doug Skinner
Guerneville, CA: Black Scat Books, 2015
DOP: August 31, 2015
Trade ppb; 220 pp.
[6 x 0.6 x 9 inches]

Note: This novel was originally published in France in 1899 by the Revue Blanche under the title *L'Affaire Blaireau*. This is the first English edition.

80.

D. Harlan Wilson, *Three Plays by D. Harlan Wilson*
Guerneville, CA: Black Scat Books, 2016
DOP: January 30, 2016
Trade ppb; 160 pp.
[5.1 x 0.4 x 7.8 inches]

81.

Derek Pell, *Missing Mysteries: A Pictorial History of Nonexistent Mysteries*

With an introduction by Llewelyn C. Hemmings
Guerneville, CA: Black Scat Books, 2016
DOP: February 25, 2016
Trade ppb; illustrated in color; 196 pp.
[8.5 x 0.5 x 11 inches]

Note: The author's handwritten annotated copy is in the collection of Jason E. Rolfe in Canada. A second printing corrected two errors in the text.

82.
Terri Lloyd, *When I Grow Up and Other Mantras*
Guerneville, CA: Black Scat Books, 2016
DOP: March 30, 2016
Trade ppb; full color plates; 174 pp.
[8.5 x 0.4 x 11 inches]

Note: The image on page 45 was published as a poster in the Black Scat Broadside series (#5).

83.
Doug Skinner, *Sleepytime Cemetery: 40 Stories*
Guerneville, CA: Black Scat Books, 2016
DOP: April 28, 2016
Trade ppb; 208 pp.
[5.1 x 0.5 x 7.8 inches]

84.
Adrienne Auvray, *Pissoirs, Bidets, Crappers & Thrones*
With an introduction by Thomas P. Ünterbottom
Guerneville, CA: Black Scat Books, 2016

DOP: May 1, 2016
Paper; color photographs; 64 pp.
[5¼ x 8¼ inches] OP

85.
P. G. Wodehouse, *A Damsel in Distress*
Illustrated by Allen Forrest
Guerneville, CA: Black Scat Books, 2016
DOP: May 25, 2016
Trade ppb; illustrated; 334 pp.
[5.1 x 0.8 x 7.8 inches]

86.
Eckhard Gerdes, *Three Plays by Eckhard Gerdes*
Guerneville, CA: Black Scat Books, 2016
DOP: June 13, 2016
Trade ppb; 132 pp.
[5.1 x 0.3 x 7.8 inches]

Note: *'S a Bird* appeared as a chapbook in the Black Scat Classic Interim Edition series. (See page 28, item #41)

87.
Norman Conquest, ed., *Oulipo Pornobongo: Anthology of Erotic Wordplay*
Guerneville, CA: Black Scat Books, 2016
DOP: July 1, 2016
Trade ppb; illustrated, color; 168 pp.
[5.1 x 0.4 x 7.8 inches]

Note: The contents of this book originally appeared in three limited edition chapbooks: *Oulipo Pornobongo,* Absurdist Texts & Documents #4 (2012), *Oulipo Pornobongo 2,* Absurdist Texts & Documents Interim edition #03 (2013), *Oulipo Pornobongo 3,* Absurdist Texts & Documents #29 (2014).

This edition includes contributions by Alphonse Allais, Alain Arias-Misson, Paulo Brito, Norman Conquest, Rusty Cuffs, Farewell Debut, Tom La Farge, Larry Fondation, Paul Forristal, Ryan Forsythe, Eckhard Gerdes, Harold Jaffe, Roger Leatherwood, D.S. Macpherson, Samantha Memi, Ellen Nations, Opal Louis Nations, Andy O'Clancy, Lance Olsen, Derek Pell, Shane Roeschlein, Thaddeus Rutkowski, Maria Schurr, Lucy Selleck, Kebob G. Shoon, Doug Skinner, Tara Stillions Whitehead, Giovanni Zuniga.

88.
Honorè de Balzac, *Waiting for Godeau*
Translated from the French by Mark Axelrod
Guerneville, CA: Black Scat Books, 2016
DOP: July 13, 2016
Trade ppb; 154 pp.
[5.1 x 0.4 x 7.8 inches]

Note: This play was originally presented in Paris at the Theatre du Gymnase-Dramatique on August 24, 1851. A limited edition of this play was published in the Absurdist Texts & Documents series (#22) in 2013.

89.
Alain Arias-Mission, *Autobiography of a Character from Fiction*
Guerneville, CA: Black Scat Books, 2016
DOP: July 27, 2016
Trade ppb; 214 pp.
[5.1 x 0.5 x 7.8 inches]

____

Second Edition
Contains an afterword by Yuriy Tarnawsky.

90.

Doug Rice, *Here Lies Memory: A Pittsburgh Novel*
Guerneville, CA: Black Scat Books, 2016
DOP: September 7, 2016
Trade ppb; illustrated with photographs by the author; 316 pp.
[6 x 0.8 x 9 inches]

91.

Amelie Walker, *Stories for Someone*
Illustrated by the author
Guerneville, CA: Black Scat Books, 2016
DOP: Nov. 24, 2106
Trade ppb; illustrated; 162 pp.
[5.1 x 0.4 x 7.8 inches]

92.

Mark Axelrod, *Superman in America & Other Absurd Plays*
Guerneville, CA: Black Scat Books, 2017
DOP: February 9, 2017
Trade ppb; 354 pp.
[5.1 x 0.9 x 7.8 inches]

93.

Alphonse Allais, *I Am Sarcey*
Compiled & Translated by Doug Skinner
Guerneville, CA: Black Scat Books, 2017
DOP: March 7, 2017
Trade ppb; 316 pp.

[5.1 x 0.6 x 7.8 inches]

Note: Portions of the book first appeared in the chapbook *How I Became an Idiot by Francisque Sarcey*, Absurdist Texts & Documents Interim Edition #00. This trade paper edition features a drawing of Allais by Sacha Guitry. and a drawing of Sarcey by Albert Guillaume.

94
Alain Arias-Mission, *The Detective Who Didn't Have a Clue*
Guerneville, CA: Black Scat Books, 2017
DOP: May 11, 2017
Trade ppb; 170 pp.
[5.1 x 0.4 x 7.8 inches]

95.
Doug Skinner, *The Doug Skinner Songbook*
Guerneville, CA: Black Scat Books, 2017
DOP: August 29, 2017
Trade ppb; 116 pp.
[8.5 x 0.3 x 11 inches]

96.
Carla M. Wilson, *Curious Impossibilities*
With an introduction by James R. Hugunin
Guerneville, CA: Black Scat Books, 2017
DOP: September 25, 2017
Trade ppb; 136 pp.
[6 x 0.3 x 9 inches]

97.
Alphonse Allais, *Long Live Life!*
Translated from the French by Doug Skinner
With an introduction, notes and illustrations by
Doug Skinner
Guerneville, CA: Black Scat Books, 2017
DOP: November 20, 2017
[6 x 0.5 x 9 inches]

Note: This collection was originally published in France in 1892 under the
title *Vive la vie!* This is the First Publication in English.

98.
Norman Conquest, ed., *Le Scat Noir Encyclo-
paedia*
Guerneville, CA: Black Scat Books, 2017
DOP: December 2, 2017
Trade ppb; illustrated; 116 pp.
[5.1 x 0.3 x 7.8 inches]

Note: This title constitutes volume 83, number 230 of the monthly journal
Le Scat Noir.

99.
Jason Rolfe, *Clocks*
Guerneville, CA: Black Scat Books, 2018
DOP: January 5, 2018
Trade ppb; 306 pp.
[5.1 x 0.8 x 7.8 inches]
Note: Some of these stories first appeared in *Le Scat Noir* and the author's
collection *An Inconvenient Corpse* (Absurdist Texts & Documents Series
#30).

100.

Doug Skinner, *The Snowman Three Doors Down*
Guerneville, CA: Black Scat Books, 2018
DOP: March 21, 2018
Trade ppb; 246 pp.
[5.1 x 0.6 x 7.8 inches]

Part IV.

New Urge Editions

101.
Cody Kmoch, *White Fire & Other Tales*
Fairfield, CA: Black Scat Books, 2015
New Urge Editions – NU-101
Trade ppb; 182 pp.
[5 x 7.7 inches] OP

Note: This is the first title published under the New Urge imprint. It features eleven erotic stories by UK writer Cody Kmoch. From the book's description: *"... sensual—often startling—sapphic stories reveal an innovative imagination...a quirky, dark sensibility that transports the reader to worlds of white fire, where fantasies, love, and sex unite. She stirs suspense and desire with a voice that is fresh and compelling."*

102.
Catherine D'Avis, *Angel of Everything*
Fairfield, CA: Black Scat Books, 2015
New Urge Editions – NU-102
Trade ppb; 138 pp.
[5 x 7.7 inches]

103.
Catherine D'Avis, *Erotic Tales*
Fairfield, CA: Black Scat Books, 2015
New Urge Editions – NU-103
Trade ppb; 162 pp.
[5 x 7.7 inches]

Note: Includes an interview with Catherine D'Avis by Terrence Welford.

____

Third Printing: June 2017

104.
Norman Conquest, ed., *The New Urge Reader: Erotic Fiction by New Women Writers*
Fairfield, CA: Black Scat Books, 2015
New Urge Editions – NU-104
Trade ppb; 146 pp.
[5.1 x 7.8 inches]

Contributors: Emily June Brink, Suzanne Burns, Catherine D'Avis, Rachel Kendall, Cody Kmoch, Pamela Naruta, L T O'Rourke, Maria Schurr, Star Spider, L C Wilkinson.

105.
Leopold von Sacher-Masoch, *Venus in Furs*
Illustrations by Nelly Sanchez
Fairfield, CA: Black Scat Books, 2015
New Urge / Classics of Passion
Trade ppb; illustrated; 234 pp.
[5.1 x 7.8 inches]

106.
Lawrence Hamilton, ed., *Hidden Gems: The Best of The Pearl, A Journal of Facetiae & Voluptuous Reading*
Fairfield, CA: Black Scat Books, 2015
New Urge / Classics of Passion
Trade ppb; 334 pp.
[5.1 x 7.8 inches]

107.
John Cleland, *Fanny Hill: Memoirs of a Woman of Pleasure*
Fairfield, CA: Black Scat Books, 2015
New Urge / Classics of Passion
Trade ppb; 310 pp.
[5.1 x 7.8 inches] OP

108.
Anonymous, *Peculiar Charms: A Victorian Erotic Novel*
Fairfield, CA: Black Scat Books, 2015
New Urge / Classics of Passion
Trade ppb; 710 pp.
[5.1 x 7.8 inches]

109.
Norman Conquest, ed., *The New Urge Reader 2: Erotic Fiction by New Women Writers*
Introduction by Elizabeth Yoo
Fairfield, CA: Black Scat Books, 2015
New Urge Editions – NU-104

Trade ppb; 178 pp.
[5.1 x 7.8 inches]

Contributors include Jessica Alexander, Tina V. Cabrera, Catherine D'Avis, Elna Holst, Eurydice Kamvyselli, Lily Knol, Marina Kris, Pamela Naruta, Erin Pim, Val Prozorova, Amy Summers, Tara Stillions Whitehead.

110.

Pierre Louÿs, *The New Pleasure & other stories*
Translated from the French by G. F. Monkshood
Guerneville, CA: Black Scat Books, 2016
New Urge / Classics of Passion
Trade ppb; 224 pp.
[5.1 x 7.8 inches]

111.

Tom Bussmann, *Sister Carrie Came*
Guerneville, CA: Black Scat Books, 2017
New Urge Editions – NU-108
Trade ppb; 144 pp.
[5.1 x 7.8 inches] OP

112.

Stephanie Gatos (Steve Katz), *Posh: An Erotical Novel*
Guerneville, CA: Black Scat Books, 2017
New Urge Editions – NU-109
Trade ppb; 192 pp.
[5.1 x 7.8 inches]

Note: "Stephanie Gatos" is a pseudonym for Steve Katz, author of *The Exaggerations of Peter Prince* and other novels. This title is a reprint of the original edition published by Grove Press in 1971.

113.
Norman Conquest and Petra Anne Hawk, eds.,
*The New Urge Reader 3: Erotic Fiction by New
Women Writers*
Introduction by Petra Anne Hawk
Guerneville, CA: Black Scat Books, 2017
New Urge Editions – NU-110
Trade ppb; 178 pp.
[5.1 x 7.8 inches]

Contributors include Tamara Faith Berger, Elizabeth Bolton, Emma Gibb,
Petra Anne Hawk, Marina Kris, Mandy Lee, Karen Moller, Pamela Naruta,
Marina Rubin, Aurora Seymour, Sophia Smith, Rebecca Woolston.

114.
John Diamond-Nigh, *Sacred Sins: Short
Sensual Stories*
Guerneville, CA: Black Scat Books, 2017
New Urge Editions – NU-111
Trade ppb; 150 pp.
[5.1 x 7.8 inches]

Addendum

Black Scat Review

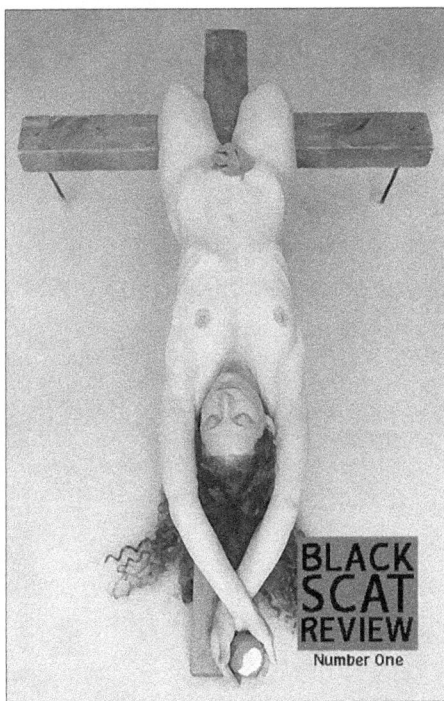

The first issue of *Black Scat Review* was published Nov. 20, 2012, featuring a controversial cover photograph by S. N. Jacobson. The magazine appeared irregularly until its final issue, No. 17 ("Dada Forgery"), Jan. 7, 2017.

Number 17 – DADA FORGERY (2017)

Contributors: Captain Anonymous, David Moscovich, Tristan Tzara, Anna Keeler, Christy Sheffield Sanford, Karl Waldmann, Ruth Crossman, Norman Conquest, Paulo Brito, Harry McCullagh, Michael Leigh, Gregory Autry Wallace, Eîlot Tuerie, Terri Lloyd, Doug Skinner, and Joseph Heathcott. 52 pp. perfect-bound, full color.

Number 16 – OBSESSION (2016)

Contributors: Alphonse Allais, Adrienne Auvray, Paulo Brito, Violet Capers, S.C. Delaney, Tony Duvert, Farewell Debut, William L. Gibson, Rachel Greenberg, Arya F. Jenkins, Samantha Memi, Agnès Potier, Mercie Pedro e Silva, Doug Skinner, and Greg Autry Wallace. 56 pp. perfect-bound, full color.

Number 15 — MORE UTTER NONSENSE (2016)

Contributors: Edward Ahern, Paulo Brito, Giada Cattaneo, Norman Conquest, Charles Cros, Falconhead, Farewell Debut, Jhaki M.S. Landgrebe, Michael Leigh, Jason E. Rolfe, Mercie Pedro e Silva, Doug Skinner, and Carla M. Wilson. Perfect-bound, full color, 78 pp.

Number 14 – PURE LUST (2016)

Contributors: Tosh Berman, Tom Bussmann, Theodore Carter, Giada Cattaneo, Elna Holst, Monika Mori, Derek Pell, Eugene Schacht, Sybil Shwarzenberg, Mercie Pedro e Silva, Yuriy Tarnawsky, Mylene Viger, Tom Whalen, and Elizabeth Yoo. Perfect-bound, illustrated, full color, 98 pp.

Note: This issue was released on March 9, 2016 and featured a red cover with an illustration by Giada Cattaneo. On March 25–without explanation – Amazon blocked sales of the issue and the printer listed it as "suppressed." A few days later, the publisher employed an alternate printer and republished it with a black cover stating "CENSORED BY AMAZON." Although no explanation was ever given for the suppression, the publisher believes it was do to an inside photograph by Mylene Viger showing an enlarged view of a woman's nipple. The original red cover is extremely rare.

Number 13 – SUPERSTITION (2015)

Contributors: Paulo Brito, Eckhard Gerdes, Harold Jaffe, Soren James, Rick Krieger, Terri Lloyd, Monika Mori, Alice Pulaski, Frank Pulaski, Doug Skinner, Mylene Viger, Dominic Ward, Carla M. Wilson. 5.06 x 7.81 inches; Trade paper; Perfect-Bound. Full color. 72 pp.

[There was no issue #12]

Number 11 (2015)

Alphonse Allais, Sandra Boersma, S. C. Delaney, Tony Duvert, Margie Franzen, William L. Gibson, Kristien Hemmerechts, Andy Koopmans, Richard Kostelanetz, Terri Lloyd, Happy Nightmares, L T O'Rourke, Derek Pell, Bobby Phillips, Agnès Potier, Thaddeus Rutkowski, Nelly Sanchez, Doug Skinner, Mark Stewart, Yuriy Tarnawsky, and Carla M. Wilson. 5.06 x 7.81 inches; Trade paper; perfect-bound. Full color, 116 pp.

Number 9/10 Special Double Issue — UTTER NONSENSE (2014)

Contributors: Jake Alexander, Alphonse Allais, Alain Arias-Misson, Mark Axelrod, Paulo Brito, Norman Conquest, Farewell Debut, Fiona Duffin, Tom La Farge, Allen Forrest, Ryan Forsythe, Eckhard Gerdes, Rhys Hughes, Janne Karlsson, Teri Lee Kline, Richard Kostelanetz, Jhaki M.S. Landgrebe, Michael Leigh, Terri Lloyd, David Macpherson, Samantha Memi, Monika Mori, Yarrow Paisley, Sheila Pell, Jason E. Rolfe, Doug Skinner, Wendy Walker, Carla M. Wilson, and D. Harlan Wilson. 5¼" x 8¼", Perfect-Bound. Full color. 128 pp.

Number 8 — SEDUCTION (2014)

Contributors: Suzanne Burns, Doug Rice, Steven Teref, Kurt Cline, Charles Holdefer, Doug Skinner, Paulo Brito, Jhaki M.S. Landgrebe, Tara Stillions Whitehead, Maria Morisot, Fox Harvard, Charlie Griggs, Monika Mori, Tom Whalen. 5¼" x 8¼", Perfect-Bound. Full color. 70 pp.

Number 7 — LIT NOIR (2014)

Contributors: Kelli Stanley, J. Kingston Pierce, Michael Hemmingson, John Nickle, Farewell Debut, Steven M. Markow, Michelle Gray, Larry Fondation, Carla M. Wilson, Susan Siegrist, Tom Larsen, Harold Jaffe, Peter Cherches, Monika Mori, and Mark Klein. 5¼" x 8¼", Perfect-Bound. Full color. 80 pp.

Number 6 (2014)

Contributors: Nin Andrews, Emily June Brink, Eckhard Gerdes, Michelle Gray, Judson Hamilton, Sarah

Katharina Kayß, Adam Miller, Ivan de Monbrison, Jules Moy, Opal Louis Nations, Doug Skinner, Brett Stout, Joanna C. Valente, Sayuri Yamada.
<< Interview with Yuriy Tarnawsky >> 5¼" x 8¼", Perfect-Bound. Full color. 78 pp.

Number 5 (2013)
Contributors: Alphonse Allais; Mark Axelrod; Andy O'Clancy; Shane Roeschlein; Samy Sfoggia; Doug Skinner; Nile Southern; Brett Stout; Patrizia Valduga. 5¼" x 8¼", Perfect-Bound. Full color, 86 pp.

Number 4 — ALL URGES GO HAYWIRE (2013)
Contributors: Alain Arias-Misson; Poggio Bracciolini; Peter Cherches; Eurydice; Pippa Anais Gaubert; Harold Jaffe; Ryan Loren Kantor; Francis Kelly; Samantha Memi; Frank Pulaski; Doug Rice; Yuriy Tarnawsky; 5¼ x 8¼ inches. Perfect-bound. Full color, 66 pp.

Number 3 (2013)
Contributors: Alphonse Allais; Erik Belgum; F. Caradec; Farewell Debut; Larry Fondation; Peter Hanssen; David Macpherson; Jim McMenamin; Opal Louis Nations; Doug Skinner; Nile Southern; Tom Whalen; Carla Wilson. 5¼ x 8¼inches. Perfect-Bound. Full color, 70 pp.

Number 2 — PLEASURE (2013)
Alain Arias-Misson; Jonathan Baumbach; Guy R. Beining; Eleanor Bennett; Miggs Burroughs; Pierre Henri Cami; John Crombie; Farewell Debut; Jacinta

Escudos; Stephen D. Gutierrez; Harold Jaffe; Richard Kostelanetz; Terri Lloyd; Samantha Memi; Opal Louis Nations; Derek Pell; Doug Skinner; D. Harlan Wilson; 5¼ x 8¼ inches. Perfect-bound. Full color, 78 pp.

Number 1 (2012)

Alphonse Allais; Elizabeth Archer; Florence Bocherel; Pierre Henri Cami; Pedro Carolino; Norman Conquest; John Crombie; S.N. Jacobson; Crad Kilodney; Michael Leigh; Samantha Memi; Doug Skinner; Yuriy Tarnawsky; Tom Whalen. 5¼ x 8¼ inches. Perfect-bound, color, 44 pp. OUT OF PRINT

Photo Gallery

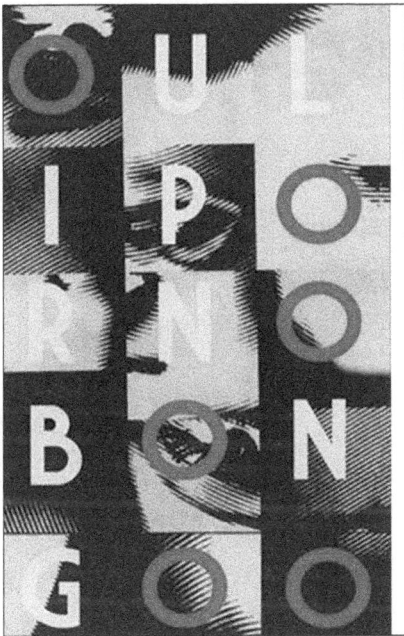

Oulipo Pornobongo: Special Edition (2012)
[See page 14, item #4]

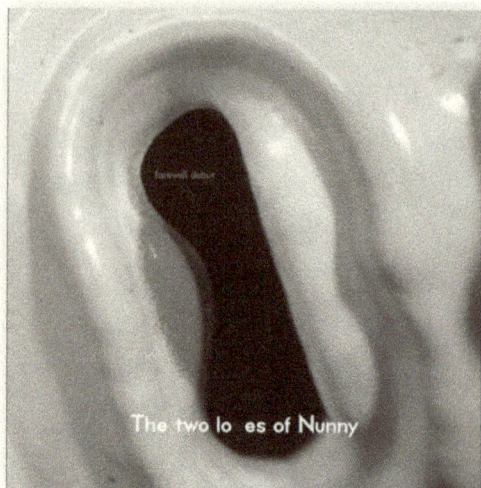

Farewell Debut, *The Two Loves of Nunny* (2012)
[See page 30, item #47]

Norman Conquest, *Snowdrop in Africa : Special Edition* (2012)
[See page 15, item #6]

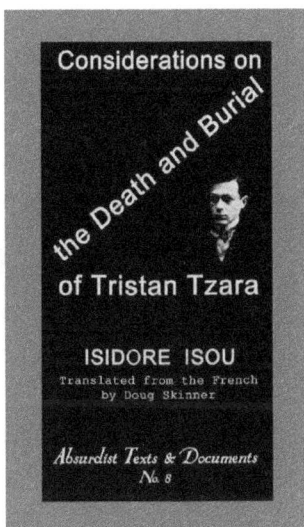

Isidore Isou, *Considerations on the
Death and Burial of Trstan Tzara* (2012)
[See page 16, item #8]

Alphonse Allais, *Captain Cap: The Sanatorium of the Future* (2012)
[See page 20, item #20]

G. Mackenzie Bacon, M.D., *Wasted Energies, Baffled Thoughts: On the Writing of the Insane*
[See page 19, item #16]

John Nickle, *Nickle Noir: The Art of John Nickle* (2013)
[See page 33, item #57]

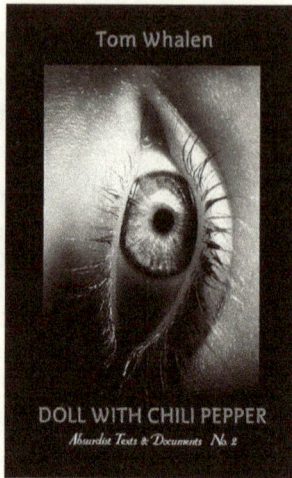

Tom Whalen, *Doll with Chili Pepper*
[See page 14, item #2]

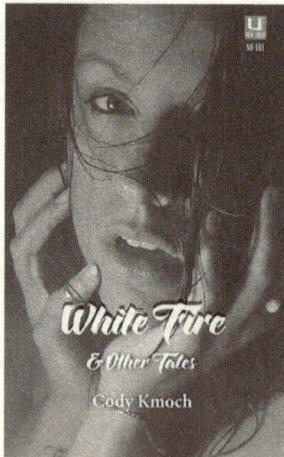

Cody Kmoch, *White Fire & Other Tales* (2015)
[See page 48, item #101]

Some Black Scat Authors

Index of Authors

R

Rice, Doug 38, 44
Rolfe, Jason E. 23
Rosheim, Paul 29

S

Sacher-Masoch, Leopold von 49
Skinner, Doug 21, 23, 35, 39, 41, 45
Slavit, David R. 22
Southern, Terry 17

T

Tarnawsky, Yuriy 34

W

Waldmann, Karl 23
Walker, Amelie 44
Wexelblatt, Robert 28
Whalen, Tom 14, 19, 35
Wilson, Carla M. 40, 45
Wilson, D. Harlan 40
Wodehouse, P. G. 42
Wood, Edward D. 22

Grace Murray attends the University of Massachusetts, Amherst where she studies English and Scandinavian Studies. She lives in Amherst with her partner and two geckos, Kiki and Lady Jane.

A checklist of JEF titles

JEF
Journal of
Experimental
Fiction